C. O Boring

Christmas mystery

C. O Boring

Christmas mystery

ISBN/EAN: 9783741192234

Manufactured in Europe, USA, Canada, Australia, Japa

Cover: Foto ©Thomas Meinert / pixelio.de

Manufactured and distributed by brebook publishing software
(www.brebook.com)

C. O Boring

Christmas mystery

A CHRISTMAS ✠ MYSTERY

I AM COME THAT YE MIGHT HAVE LIFE.

BY CHARLES O. BORING

CHICAGO.
THE FORWARD MOVEMENT PUBLISHING CO.
1896.

DEDICATION.

This little book is dedicated by the author to THE FOR-WARD MOVEMENT, as representative of the new spirit man-ifested in the uplift of humanity by the helpful association and close touch of consecrated lives.

The social movement indicated by the various settlements, of which this is a type, is the characteristic Christ-like feature of this generation.

The influence coming from this work, and the added suggestions of the teaching of co-operation, which is the essential spirit of this work, are encouraging proofs that just before us is the dawn of a new day.

All profits arising from the sale of this book, are sacredly dedicated to The Forward Movement.

CHARLES O. BORING.

CHICAGO, NOVEMBER 13, 1896.

815298

A Christmas Mystery.

I NEVER knew why I was belated on that evening. It was already dark, and the electric lights, gleaming from the street corners, lit up the faces of those passing along, and I saw, from all the signs; that this was an unusual evening. Nearly every one bore bundles of some sort, on all the faces was a glow of expectancy, and from these evidences I knew that this was Christmas eve.

Passing in deep meditation, I was thinking what this day meant to me. It had always been a marvelous day in the history of my life, and more than once I had received, on this anniversary, some new and wonderful revelation.

Filled with these thoughts, as I suddenly turned a corner, I saw before me a scene of glorious splendor. There, rising majestically into the air, was an edifice, which was indeed, like a dream. It was a miracle of brightness, there did not seem to be a shadow about it. The light came from within, from without, from above, from beneath. It glowed like a corruscation, or rather, as if it were a living, luminous being. Was the Taj Mahal, Pearl of India, magnified and glorified, transported by some miracle to this place?

What was the material of which this was builded? Its surface, where not luminous from within, seemed of some brilliant, white metal, which might be aluminum if such were possible.

Just before me was a splendid portal. Over that portal, in darkened characters against the bright, white light, I read these words: I AM COME THAT YE MIGHT HAVE LIFE. Above this inscription was a figure moulded or carved from some translucent substance. The light gleamed through the golden hair, it shone out of the blue eyes and through the light drapery, as though this were indeed a living person, so strangely life-like did it appear. The arms were outstretched, and in the face looking down upon those beneath, I saw the face of my Redeemer.

As I stood gazing in bewilderment, at this marvelous structure, I could not help saying to myself: "I never saw this before! how strange, I never saw this before!"

A young man was standing by my side, looking upon the throng of people pressing into the portal and gathered about the promenade around this great edifice. As he heard these words from my lips he turned and said to me: "Why do you say that it is strange you have never seen this before?"

I replied: "Nearly all my life has been passed in this city. I have been a constant observer of all events of importance, and yet I have never seen this building, neither have I ever heard a word about it.",

"How long have you been living here?' said he.

"I have lived in or about Chicago more than thirty years."

"Your statement is unaccountable," the young man said, "I have been acquainted with this building all my life, and I did not know that there was any one, in all the world—much less in Chicago— who did not know of its existance."

"What is the building?" I asked, "what is the purpose of it; what do they call it"

"I should think," he said, "you would at once see

what it is. Notice the stained windows, with the
pictures limned upon them? Observe these groups of
statues, one above the other to the very top-most
height of the building!"

"Yes" I replied, "I read in all these tokens that old
familiar and beautiful story of the life of our Savior."

"You are right," said he, "and this is the CHURCH OF
THE REDEEMER. I am glad to say there are many
scattered over the world, and also others in this city
not like it in architecture, or in beauty, for in these
respects it is yet supreme, but they are similar in
spirit, and that after all is the best resemblance."

"Tell me, how did this great enterprise come about?
Who originated it?"

"I have often heard my father speak of it, and
know the story well. No man originated it. It was
the product of the age, the ripened thought of the
centuries. This thought localized the CHURCH in
Chicago, because of an event in this city, but it may
truly be said, that all the world participated in its
inauguration, and all the past in its inception."

"You remember" he continued, "the Columbian Ex-
position and the effect it had upon Chicago and the
world. You also remember the Parliament of Relig-
ions, and you know too the marvelous influence which

went forth from this. THIS CHURCH is the sequence of both of these significant events."

"The business men of Chicago, who were more than mere men of business, and who had been moved out of the ruts of dogmatic thinking, by the impetus given through that initiative, resolved that those great object lessons should not be lost. They proposed to perpetuate, in some form, the thought which had come to the world, of beauty, of art, of architecture, of spiritual life, and especially, of brotherhood. The evolution of this idea was first seen in the lavish donations, to furnish means for its construction, which poured in without solicitation from everywhere and from persons of all grades of thought and religious opinions. When the spirit of giving was started, it seemed as if it would never cease. That which had begun as a comparitively small thing, grew until the result was the majestic Temple which you see occupying yonder entire square.

"There was no thought of calling this a church, when the idea was first proposed, but when the architect presented the plan, it was seen that it could be nothing else, and so it was then named, and has been called ever since THE CHURCH OF THE REDEEMER.

"Of what denomination is it?"

"Denomination! What do you mean by that term

6

I do not understand it?"

"Of what sect is it?" I asked.

"Oh," he replied, "I have heard my father speak of
such things and I recollect what you mean. We now
know nothing of what used to be called denom-
inations or sects, and we can hardly realize that
any one would use such terms."

"What has become of the old churches? Are they
abandoned or destroyed?"

"They have been absorbed," said the young man,
"into many enterprises. Some of the buildings remain
and are in use, but not many. They were not
valuable for the new purposes and were generally
removed. The readjustment was brought about
gradually at first, but rapidly at the close."

"What has become of the property rights which
the statutes recognized as being vested in the denom-
inations?"

The young man laughed heartily and was scarcely
able to speak for a moment. Then he said,
"Please excuse me, but I remember reading sometime
since, a book named 'THE RUINS OF GOD'S TEMPLES,'
written after the movement had commenced, by one
who had not come into this new fellowship.
It called attention to the doleful fact of the abandon-

ment of the down-town churches for the CHURCH OF THE REDEEMER, and claimed because of this, the city was hopelessly lost to religion and to God."

"Were these churches really abandoned?" said I.

"In fact they were. The properties were so tied up by the old legal enactments that they could not be utilized and in consequence simply stood idle for a time."

"Is it so now?" I inquired, for I was determined to see how this strange jest would terminate. I fully realized that this young man had a most unusual faculty of humor, and that he recognized me as a proper victim for a joke. To encourage him however, I continued; "How did this feature terminate or has it indeed ended?"

"Certainly it has ended, and the ending was very beautiful."

"It had been a principle long established, that church property should pay no taxes to state or city. This principle was finally of the greatest service; for, because of it, the state finally claimed this abandoned property as belonging to the people."

"Was there not a good deal of trouble arising out of this?" I replied; as I was now fully determined to carry this comedy to its close.

"Far from it," the young man said. "The harmony which came out of the birth and early development of the CHURCH OF THE REDEEMER fully prevented any such thought. When the principle of co-operation which this fellowship taught, was established the result was that rivalries ceased. People began to think together and then to work together and the result was that there was no possible cause for jealousy or rivalry."

I was becoming so confused that I hardly knew what to say. The young man appeared truthful and it was evident one of us was laboring under a great delusion.

I now began to notice the statuary upon the building, and saw that it was superior to any I had ever before observed. The young man looked at me curiously, seeing my eager scrutiny, but said nothing.

"Tell me," said I; "how do the people feel about these images so numerous upon this building?"

"Truly," he replied, "you have just touched upon a point which was in great controversy for a long time. However, the competition of the artists of the world, to produce this great assemblage of statues, brought such a return of the old Christ art, of Raphael and Michael Angelo, that it absolutely revolutionized Christian sentiment upon the subject."

"It is strange to me that such transformations should come to pass and that I should be ignorant of them."

"Strange," the young man said, "I cannot understand it. I do not know where you could have been and not know of this. There is nothing so much talked of in the world, and to-night, while we are standing here, they are everywhere reading of the prepartions going on for the festival which shall be held in this place, to night."

I now began to notice the great throng of people which seemed to come from every direction, and which was pouring in at the open portal just before me. One thing which especially attracted my attention at this time, was the number of ladies unattended by escorts.

I asked my young friend if this was not unusual. He looked at me in astonishment.

"Why should they fear anything?" said he.

"But," I answered, "are they not in danger of insult from the gamblers or saloon attendants?"

In still greater bewilderment, he answered, "there has not been a saloon nor any institution of that kind within five miles of this church for over twenty-five years."

"Who closed them? That was indeed a wonderful work."

"The CHURCH closed them. It began a revolution in the immediate neighborhood and this extended rapidly."

"But how was this accomplished?"

"The people were won away from the evil places by the greater attractions of this CHURCH and other places of similar character elsewhere in the city. Their patronage ceased, and in fact, nearly all of them were closed even before it became unlawful to keep them open."

"But what has become of the wild fellows who used to visit them?"

"They were among the very first to yield. These made some of our noblest men, and you could not now attract them to such a place as the saloon used to be. There was a jubilee when the last resort in the heart of the city was closed. The young man laughed again and apologized by saying that he so seldom had heard the word I had just mentioned that he was not sure but that he might entirely have forgotten it, but for a curious blunder of the author of the book on the RUINED TEMPLES, which he had referred to before. This author confounded the old word 'saloon' with the word *Salon*, which was used considerably at that time in some of the entertainments at the CHURCH OF THE REDEEMER."

"You must certainly read this book," said the young man. "It is out of print, but there is a copy in the library in the church, and it will pay you sometime to stop and examine it in order that you may see what fear our fore-fathers had to conquer."

Just at this moment I saw a newsboy passing, with his bundle of papers under his arm, and crying the sale of "Redeeming News." I bought a copy of the paper. I saw upon the front of it a splendid picture of this wonderful memorial institution, but I saw something also which startled me, so that I was not able to speak in answer to the question of the young man who stood beside me. Upon the head-lines were these words: *"December 24th, 1949."*

While I was endeavoring to gather my thought and bring myself into some recognition of the time and the place, and was trying to recall what had happened since December 22, 1892, the date I last remembered, I heard strange sounds from across the street. The young man touched my arm and said, "Come, here is a Romany boy, let us go and hear him play."

Dazed with the intense excitement of conflicting

emotions, I crossed the broad street and the wide esplanade, which surrounded the building, and there, near one of the great pillars, was a lad of about eighteen years. He was bareheaded and his long, raven locks curled luxuriantly over his shoulders. His white face was turned to the sky, and I saw that the orbs were sightless. He played an instrument, the like of which I had never seen. It was a sort of portable pipe organ, capable no doubt in skilled hands, of marvelous effects of music; but here was more than skill. This was a born musician, whose very soul was pouring itself forth. One wise in such matters would know from his manner of playing that he was a "Tsigane," who had learned in that wild, weird school of nature-students, a method, which those who have been trained in the mere technicalities of music, can never acquire. His was evidently not mere learning. It was a deeper knowledge, a true spiritual hearing and revealing of the music of the invisible world. His soul was engrossed in the rhapsody, so that he seemed to know not where he was or what he was doing. The coins dropped in the little box, at the end of his strange instrument, but he heeded them not. It was the "Czarda" which filled his soul, and only that.

The crowd which had gathered close about him now parted, as an elderly man with long, white hair,

made his way to the side of the blind boy and listened for a few moments to this strange, wild improvisation.

His face was beautiful in its outward form and bore a look of benevolence apparently characteristic of it, but a more glorious expression irradiated it as he stood there, as if from an internal illumination.

Like the blind boy he, too, seemed transported in spirit to some far away realm where only harmonious vibrations were realized. The world of mortal sense was lost to him, as well, and he met in Paradise, the one whom he had outwardly seen but a moment before at the church portal.

Suddenly he became conscious of his position, for the throng parted on either side of him, and left him fully revealed in the bright radiance which streamed through the window, before which stood the statue of the smiling Christ.

The glory which shone out of that matchless countenance was burning in this face as well. Impulsively brushing the white locks from before his eyes, and stepping up to the lad, he said, "Come with me and hear me play."

As he led him away through the portal, I asked my young acquaintance, "who is that?"

"Do you not know John Woodbridge?" he replied.

"No, who is he?"

"It is strange, I cannot understand it," he said. "I did not know there was any one, in all the world, who did not know of John Woodbridge, the great organist of THE CHURCH OF THE REDEEMER. But come, shall we not go in and I will tell you about him."

We entered the corridor, with the great throng of people which was pouring into the building and yet so quiet, so orderly were they, that there was no disturbance or the least excitement. It seemed as if some mysterious influence came upon all as soon as they entered. They passed within reverently, as if going to a place which they loved, and which they were accustomed to often visit.

We were soon in the auditorium. Surely this was a new and strange world to me. Here was a vast ampitheatre of such size, as had never been dreamed of before that day of marvels, when the great "Manufacturers' building" was planned. Not only was this so large that any other hall was a mere dwarf in comparison, but here was also a brilliancy of illumination never witnessed Gallery rose above gallery, stretching away in misty distances, and yet every part was as light as if the bright sun-light streamed

in from above, while no lamps of any kind were
in sight.

If the irradiance of the exterior was so surpassing
that it was beyond my knowledge, how much more
this resplendent glory.

When seated I looked about me. How many thousands could such a building contain? What human
voice could ever fill such an auditorium? What
music might ever be rendered there, by any instrument or assemblage of instruments however grand
that would not be lost?

My young friend seeing the look of astonishment
upon my face said, "I see that you do not compre-
hend this place at all. You cannot understand how
anything can be heard in this vast room."

"Yes," I replied, "that thought was in my mind as
you spoke."

"And yet so cunningly is this room designed that
there is not a seat in this auditorium, but the faintest
whisper from yonder platform, can reach it, and as for
the effect of music, it is as perfect as if it had been
planned for no other purpose. But soon you shall
judge for yourself, and you will hear what all the world
has been awaiting in great expectancy. It is many
years since John Woodbridge has used the great organ
and the announcement that he will perform tonight

has brought thousands from afar, even some from the remotest parts of the world. I have often heard about the last time that he played in this CHURCH. It was fourteen years ago to night, and it was said by those who were here that they had never listened to such music, neither had they ever dreamed of such possibilities of music, as came out of the grand organ under his touch. I have also heard how grievously were all shocked, when they learned the next day, that even while he was enchanting his listeners here, little Charlie, his only child, the boy upon whom the affections of his heart had centered, was stolen away from his home. John Woodbridge has passed the years in sorrow and in seeking, but he has sought in vain through all the world. At last, unasked, he has again offered his services to play this night, and you are fortunate, indeed, that you chance to be here."

"Tell me about this great instrument," and I turned my face toward one side of this spacious hall, where there arose from the lowest floor to the highest ceiling, the most majestic piece of organ architecture. No glowing, tawdry colors were anywhere put upon it to hurt and offend the eye, but soft shades like those in old tapestry, and glows, like phosphorescent lights in the forest, everywhere relumned it.

"Tell me about the organ."

"Surely" he replied, "you have heard all about this, every one knows of it."

"No; how could I hear of it, when I did not even know of the building."

"Your statements fill me with more and more wonder. There is no time to question you now, but I will tell you of the organ. Who built it? no one knows, or at least those who know will never tell the secret. It was a princely offering, like many another which was given this enterprise, and like others of these rich gifts which adorn this place, was not intended for selfish gratification through the public announcement of its donor. It is a magnificent organ as you can easily judge from its outer appearance but it is more than that, it is a miracle of power. There are other organs in the world that are grand but this surpasses them all. Strangely enough the secret of the mechanism of this instrument has never been learned. Engineers and students from all the world have come here, seeking to learn its mystery but they have never yet solved it. And there is something still more wonderful, for while it is a great organ surpassing any other, under all circumstances yet at times its superiorty is so great that it can not in the least be compared."

"At times! if at times, why not at all times?"

"Oh!" he replied, "you have not learned the mystery of which I shall speak. When this organ is played by one, who is truly an artist, but who is also spiritual, true and deep in his nature, by these means he seems to be brought into some sort of mystic relation with the one who builded it. There is then an added power and sweetness, which makes it as far surpass itself under ordinary conditions, as it at all times surpasses all others. John Woodbridge is today the only one we know of such ability, and you need not marvel as you see these multitudes pouring up through the elevators into the galleries, and streaming in through every portal. Even this great place will be altogether too small for those who wish to hear him to night."

There was no sign or note of alarm, but suddenly the vast audience was hushed, and then from one of the galleries came the voices of a thousand children singing a sweet christmas melody. There was no harsh accompaniment of instruments to destroy the richness and freshness of these delightful voices, which rang out as tuneful as the lark's voice, at early morn. Here were a thousand voices, blended into one; fresh, sweet, tender and clear When this ceased there was silence for a moment, and then from another gallery came the "Song of the Angels to the Shepherds," by a thousand male voices. When had I

heard music that had such power and pathos?
When had such masterful and soulful singing gone
from the earth to vibrate in unison with the songs of
the upper air?

Then twelve trumpeters stepped to the front of
the platform, the vast audience rose to its feet, and
led by these, joined in a grand old Christmas Hymn.

I thought I had heard the singing of multitudes
before, when it meant something, but surely never
before had I listened to anything like this: for, to culture and refinement was added a glorious potency of
sound which seemed impossible from human throats.

Ere the thought of this faded from my mind there
appeared on the platform a man of small stature and
very plain appearance.

"Who is this?" I asked.

"What!" he replied, "have you never heard of Evan
Lloyd?'

"No, I have never heard of him. Who is he?"

"Well, I will not need to tell you. He is about
to speak, and you will then know all about him."

He stood before the hushed audience and told over
that old, old story of the birth of the Redeemer.
I had heard it again and again, until it seemed as if it
were impossible that anything new should ever be

said upon the subject, but behold now, it was all new it was all fresh. It was the same story but there was an added meaning to every declaration.

I did not marvel, that, as I looked about me, I saw the misty eyes of those who were nearest me, for I felt the dew spring to my own eye-lids, and my heart was strangely moved.

Looking down the aisle, in one of the seats before me, I saw the blind boy, the recent protege of the great organist. He was leaning upon his instrument, bending forward to catch every word which came from the lips of the speaker. I read in his face that he seemed to be listening for the first time in his life, to the story of the Redeemer. The longing look upon that face portended he too wished that help, which Evan Lloyd promised to those who would take upon themselves this life. The tears poured from his sightless orbs, his hands were clasped convulsively, and I saw that he could not restrain his sobs. In a few moments his face glowed with a bright light and I then knew that the wandering youth had found a resting place in the knowledge of the Christ, and that he had taken him for Master..

The speaker ceased. There was a hush in the great hall, a quietness such as I had never felt before, then out of that stillness stole a sound, so faint, so far away—it might be the breathing of flutes upon the hilltops—it swelled and grew, and gained in power until there was such strength and sublimity of tones that it seemed that this was not mere mechanism, but the canorous unisonance of more than finite, living creatures. It was indeed as if the world were an organ and the music was filling the universe.

Truly here was a great organ, and of marvelous mechanism, but a more marvelous player. Motet and canon, quatrain, cantata, symphony and oratorio were developed in harmonious succession. The music died away until it was so still that you could hear only the far away voice of a Nightingale, that sweet and sad refrain, that stole somewhere out of the great instrument; then at last out of the comparative silence burst forth a rhapsody. I had heard it before. Yes, I recalled that it was the Czarda which the blind boy played that evening It grew in power and motive, and sank away again into silence, or nearly so, and then out of this silence came the note, clear and ringing, of a silver bell. And now over and above everything, I heard that old sweet song of the Holy Night, played in wondrous chimes of consonance, while underneath, and weaving in and out was the Czarda.

I had forgotten my surroundings, or rather

was transported on the wings of the moving wind
into the depths of the earth where I heard the rhythmic vibration of the elements. I felt the throb of the
forces which laid the foundations of the world.
Thence I was borne, until, far from the world, I
rested and listened, and caught the concordant harmony of the universe. My heart was stilled into
wondrous peace, when above all, I heard again the
voices; this time of the celestials singing the grand old
song, Peace on Earth and Good Will Among Earth's
Inhabitants. Suddenly, I was again in the CHURCH
OF THE REDEEMER, with my young companion at
my side.

As I sat there, the tears streaming from my
eyes, I felt that here was a spiritual force I had
never before known in music. There were sermons,
yes great volumes of sermons in those tones, and I
felt myself lifted above the world, and all of its
temptations. I had come to know something of the
deeper mystery of the great organ.

The little preacher, with the motion of his hand
called us to our feet and dismissed us with the ben-
ediction and the festival was over.

The audience went out of the house in silence. No
one stopped to even exchange a word with his neigh-
bor, for all felt the beautiful solemnity of the hour, and

that they had been given a revelation such as had never come to them before.

* * * *

"Come," said the young man, "perhaps you would like to know more of this church. I will show it to you."

We passed through the halls, and then from one floor to another by means of elevators. I soon saw that this was more than a place for people to meet to worship one day in the week, and a far different institution from anything of which I had knowledge. I saw that the wants of the natural as well as of the spiritual man were provided for, and that every helpful plan and thought for the betterment of body, mind and spirit were here embodied. The sublime idea of a church that reached down to the lowest and yet helped the most advanced in intellectual and spiritual life, was fully realized.

"Now shall we not hasten," I suggested, "will they not soon close the building."

He laughed as he said. "Close the building? Why this church is open every hour of the day and night and every day in the week; it stands to help all who need, and why should it ever be closed? No, the great auditorium is closed until to-morrow morning but there are hundreds of rooms that are always in use. No request is ever refused, and helpers are always here to give their assistance." Then he showed me the restaurant standing open, where those were fed without price who came to ask for food; and the sleeping rooms where they were lodged without cost, for mere asking.

"But are you never imposed upon?"

"No, that is impossible. At first it seemed as if this might be true, but it was soon learned that no one came but the distressed, and no questions are now asked except to know if there is a need, for one of our first and greatest lessons was that men could be taught to trust each other. This is what the church is for," he said, "that is the very thought of it in every way, that it shall help every one who is in want."

As we passed hastily along I was shown a large portion of the building which was set apart for offices and other commercial purposes. These I was told were rented, and the amount realized seemed to my mind an extravagantly large sum.

"I suppose," said I, "that it is by this means THE CHURCH is supported"

"Far from it. Every dollar of that money is sacredly set apart to be used in promoting like enterprises elsewhere in the world."

"But how are the expenses of THIS CHURCH provided."

"By voluntary contributions. The money is never asked for, but it always comes as it is needed. The demands of faith bring the supplies."

We stepped out upon the balcony and looked over the great lake lying at our feet, for the atmosphere was marvelously clear, and here and there I saw splendid pinacles of light, but none so wonderfully brilliant as this.

I heard the sound of voices beneath me, and looking over the balcony saw a crowd gathering at the portal of THE CHURCH.

"Come," I suggested, "let us see what this means," and we started at once to descend to the street.

Passing through the building I was surprised to see multitudes of people coming from various apartments, and asked my acquaintance what so many people were doing here at this time of the night.

"These are people," said he, "who have spent the evening in the art rooms, and departments of physical culture. Others are students of various cults and classes, and very many have spent the evening in the reading rooms and library."

"Are not these attractions closed when THE

CHURCH is open?"

My friend smiled, as if this was a strange remark.

"You and I will get to understand each other after a time," said he. "I find it very difficult to see the meaning of this question."

"Does not THE CHURCH require all other departments to be closed during its public services."

My friend appeared very merry for a moment and then replied, "You are of course aware that all do not enjoy or require the same physical food. If this is true in this lower realm, how much more is it true in the nourishment of the higher life."

"The rule of our fellowship is that no criticism shall be passed upon any one for their selection of recreation or work."

"Where are the apartments for the lower classes? I note these are all well dressed people and appear prosperous."

"Lower classes! who and what are they?"

I did not stop to answer for we had now reached the landing and hurried out to the street, to note what had occasioned the excitement we had noticed from the balcony. We learned that there had been strange occurrences in THE CHURCH that night. After the auditorium had been closed, and when all was dark within, watchmen of the building had heard the sound of the great organ: Soon they were most alarmed, for as if by some marvelous appliance hithertoo unknown, the great organ had repeated the entire *repertoire* of the evening, or else, the spirit of John Woodbridge had now returned to repeat the Christmas Melodies, given that night.

These men were bold under ordinary circumstances, but here was something so passing their knowledge, that they did not dare to enter THE CHURCH to see what the occasion of this disturbance might be. All was still within. Suddenly John Woodbridge, the the very one whose apparition they thought had been playing upon this organ, came upon the scene. They were sure no one but he, could have given these glorious renditions.

At the close of the Christmas Festival, it appeared, that John Woodbridge had started for his home at Lake Geneva, on the Elevated Electric Road. Having taken his place upon the train he soon fell into a doze, when he heard strange sounds, as if some one were trying to play upon the great organ of THE CHURCH OF THE REDEEMER. At first this attempt was uncertain, but gradually the player seemed to have gained confidence and power, until at last he had rendered every selection which he himself had given that evening, including the "Czarda" which the blind boy had played outside of THE CHURCH. He arose from his seat, and getting off at the next station, returned by the first train to Chicago.

Reinforced with his presence, the watchmen dared to enter. The great glow lights were turned on on and the auditorium was searched until there, fast asleep under the organ bench, they found the blind boy. He had been so overcome by his emotions that he had not heard the multitude passing out and had remained in solitude and silence. Then there came over him a temptation to play the organ. He stole forward to it and found the motor stop, and soon the other stops, —for his fingers were more than eyes— and began to play. At first he had no knowledge, but he soon seemed to gain it, and then he poured forth his soul upon that great instrument, as he had upon the little one in the street, except that he repeated that which he had heard, and had been to him such a marvelous revelation. He had come into a higher realm of music that night than he ever entered before and had mastered the mystery of the great organ through the greater Christmas mystery.

The watchmen were not sentimentalists, so that it was not strange that they should insist on taking the boy to the detention jail, until the question of the responsibility of using the organ was decided.

John Woodbridge said that he would go with him and I said I would go also, As we were sitting in the conveyance that was to take us to this place, the boy told us something of his story.

He only knew he was a lonely lad, although he had wandered over the world with his tribe; that he loved to be out in the open fields, and hear the song of the birds and the sighing of the wind, and every sound which nature bore into his soul. He had been taught music by his masters, but he had learned more of it by himself. He had lost his sight in some way in his earlier years, but he had not missed it much, as he had been able to go anywhere his comrades had gone.

When in far away Africa he had learned of the great organ and resolved that he should hear it for himself and was nearly a year in making his way to Chicago. At last he had heard it and had even played upon it and now his soul was supremely satisfied.

When we reached the jail, I was astonished, for I could not remember having before seen so decent and clean a place as this, used for such a purpose.

When we came to the cell to which the lad was assigned, he was overcome by the emotions through which he had passed, and fell almost unconsious into the arms of John Woodbridge, who removed his clothing carefully and tenderly as if he were his own little boy. Suddenly he started back with an exclamation of glad astonishment, and then falling on his knees, poured out his soul in thankful prayer to Almighty God.

Yes, it was his own Charlie, the boy of his heart; the one whom he had lost and who had been sent back to him so strangely this night. Now he knew why his heart warmed so to the lad, as he played outside THE CHURCH, and he knew also why he had asked him to come within THE CHURCH that he might hear him play. He knew also why he had so surpassed himself that night, and also why the theme of the Holy Night with the accompanying Czarda, had broken in upon his own soul as a breath from heaven. He and his own twice-born child, had together tasted the sweet waters, and heard the wild melodies of uttermost land, but here, reunited body and spirit, they mingled their blissful tears, as we stood, joyful witnesses of the unfolding of this sacred mystery.

Now we knew why the boy who had never learned music, as a science, had been able to do that which no one but the great organist had ever accomplished. Surely John Woodbridge had recovered his own loved boy, and THE CHURCH OF THE REDEEMER could have one to succeed him in his office, who possessed his own mysterious nature, and who was not only his child in his natural generation, but was more than ever, his child by spiritual inheritance.

My eyes filled with blinding tears as I stood looking upon this sweet and touching scene.

* * * * *

Suddenly the room in the jail had vanished, the warden, the organist, and the blind lad; all had gone into dreamland.

* * *

I heard rhythmic throbs, but these were strange sounds to me, and unremembered. I wiped the mist from my eyes that had gathered as I heard the burst of joy which came from John Woodbridge, and replacing my eye-glasses, looked about me.

* * * * *

Into what new world had I been so suddenly brought Slowly I came to earth consciousness, and again remembered my surroundings. The brakeman of the train upon which I was riding cried out the name of the station, as the train came to a halt, and I recalled that he was announcing this same stopping place as I left my body, to speed away into the Eastern realms of God's universe, where the events that will come to pass to-morrow are already written in Celestial records.

FINIS.